Origins

The WOW! Award

Chris Powling ▪ Jonatronix

OXFORD
UNIVERSITY PRESS

Greenville's most up-to-date news

GREENVILLE NEWS

Scientist X Behind Bars!

Dr X, one of the most respected scientists at NICE (National Institute for the Creation of Energy), has been arrested. Following an investigation by Inspector Textor of the Greenville City Police Department, he was taken into custody yesterday for questioning.

Shrinking Plot EXposed

It turns out that Dr X's ground-breaking work for NICE has been a cover for a more sinister operation. In his hideout underneath the NICE building, Dr X has been busy building NASTI (Nano Science and Technology Inc). NASTI has been developing a secret weapon called the X-machine. The X-machine has the power to shrink things to micro-size. Dr X intended to use his machine to shrink the world so that he could be the greatest and most powerful person in it! But unfortunately for Dr X, he was shrunk to micro-size in the process.

Thanks to the heroic exploits of four brave children, Max, Cat, Ant and Tiger, from Green Bank School, Dr X's plans have come to nothing. It is thought that the children, along with the scientist Dani Day, helped to foil Dr X's plans. Dani Day, recently promoted to Senior Scientist at NICE, managed to restore Dr X to normal size so he could be safely locked away. Although the full story has not yet been told, the children are due to be interviewed today at the famous *WOW!* magazine where all will be revealed.

Chapter 1 – A BLIP in time

The children could hardly believe their luck. They were in a long, flashy car, fit for a rock star, on their way to *WOW!*

"*WOW!* is the coolest magazine in the whole world!" exclaimed Cat, who could hardly sit still. "And they want to interview *us!*"

"Well, we did defeat Dr X," said Tiger, pushing the button to open and close the windows for the fifth time.

"They think we're heroes!" laughed Max.

"And so you are," said Max's mum, who was going with them to the magazine's head office. She had bought a new dress especially for the occasion. "I'm very proud of you."

"Thanks, Mum," said Max. "But it still seems a lot of fuss about nothing. What do you think, Ant? Do you feel like a hero?"

"Huh …?"

"Earth calling, Ant," said Max. "Come in, Ant!"

Ant wasn't listening. His eyes were fixed on his watch as he tapped away at the buttons. When Ant was in one of his thoughtful moods there was no getting through to him.

Max sighed and turned away to look out of the window. So did the others. By now Tiger was waving at all the people they passed. Max and Cat started to wave, too. Even Mum joined in.

So none of them noticed when Ant suddenly disappeared.

BLIP!

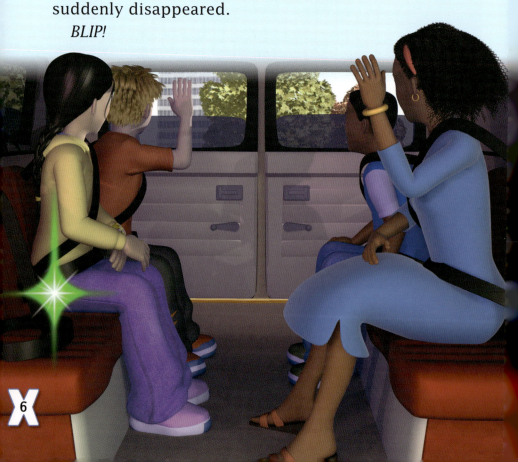

BLIP!
Just as suddenly, Ant was back again.

"Hey, you guys," he said, shakily. "I think I ... the watches, they ..."

"Not now, Ant!" Cat interrupted. "We'll be arriving at *WOW!* any moment!"

"But I think I actually ..."

"Save it till later, Ant," said Max.

"Yes, but ..."

"Look at that!" said Tiger, pointing at a big building.

"But ..."

"Hey," whooped Cat, "We're here!"

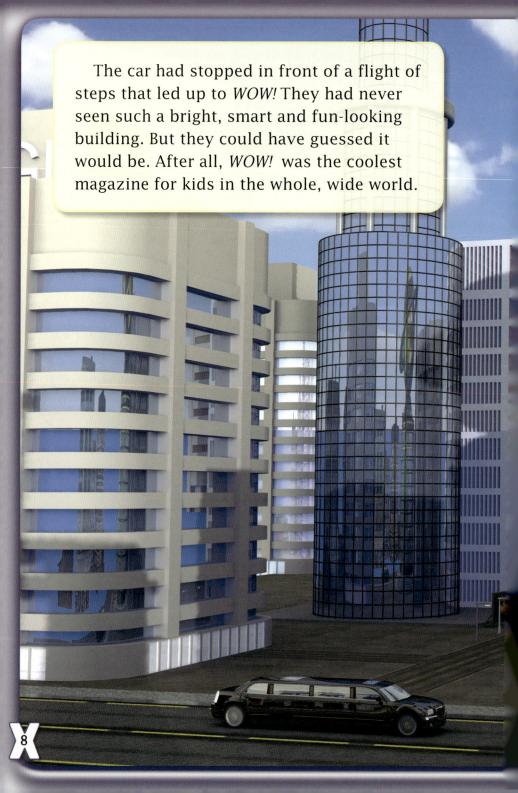

The car had stopped in front of a flight of steps that led up to *WOW!* They had never seen such a bright, smart and fun-looking building. But they could have guessed it would be. After all, *WOW!* was the coolest magazine for kids in the whole, wide world.

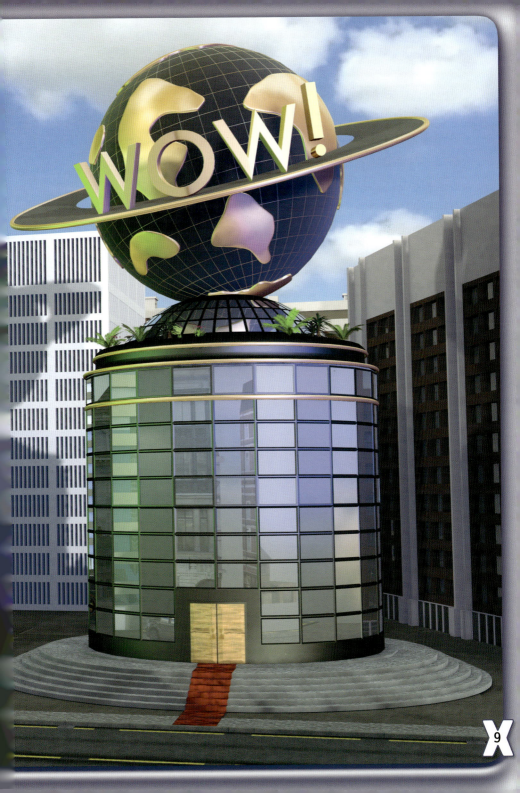

Chapter 2 – *WOW!*

They were taken straight to the editor-in-chief. Her name was Penny Piminy. She was bright, smart and fun-looking, too – just like the building.

"We're so happy you're here!" she smiled. "Just imagine! An interview with the kids who saved us from Dr X! What could be more *WOW!* than that? It's almost as exciting as our other visitor ..."

"Your other visitor?" said Cat.

"She'll be here a bit later on," said Penny. "She's the winner of this year's *WOW!* Award for being Wonderful."

"You don't mean ...?" gasped Cat.

Cat had gone starry-eyed. So had Max, Ant and Tiger. Even Max's mum was impressed. They had seen the movies. They had watched the DVDs. They had downloaded the podcasts. But best of all, they had read book after book after book.

"You announced it in your last issue," Cat whispered. "Isn't the winner ... K J Sparkling?"

"Spot on!" Penny smiled.

"Will we get to meet her?" asked Tiger eagerly.

"Maybe. But she's such a busy lady, she might not be able to stay for long. Anyway, shall we get on with your interview?" said Penny. "I want to hear all about how you got the better of Dr X!"

Before they could start, the phone on Penny's desk buzzed.

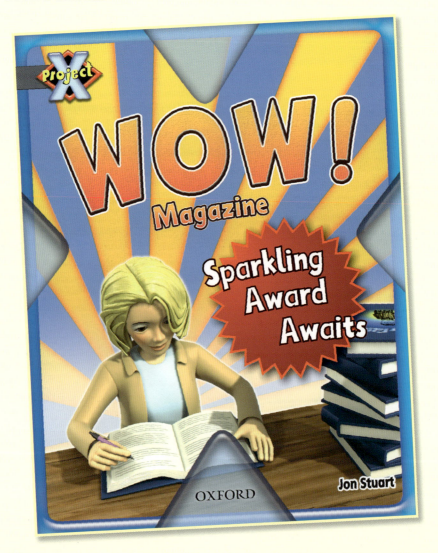

BUZZ BUZZ

Penny picked it up. As she listened, a broad grin spread across her face.

"It's your lucky day after all!" she told them. "Our other visitor has just arrived – much earlier than we expected. She's coming up in the lift. It's K J Sparkling in person!"

Chapter 3 – K J Sparkling (1)

The children recognized her at once, even though her blonde hair hid half her face. People said she was the world's shyest celebrity. And yet...

"She's shorter than I thought she'd be," whispered Tiger.

"And rounder," said Ant.

"Ssshhhhh!" hushed Cat.

K J Sparkling crossed the room. "Hi, I'm K J Sparkling. Are you Penny Piminy?" she beamed at Penny.

"Yes, I am ..."

"And who are these darling children? No, don't tell me! Are you the famous Max, Cat, Ant and Tiger? I've been *longing* to meet you, you know. I might even put you in my next book."

"Your next book?" Cat gasped.

"Us?" said Tiger.

"Why not?" said K J Sparkling. "A writer is always on the lookout for new and exciting characters. And who could be more exciting than the children who got the better of Dr X?"

The world's most famous and successful author shook each of the children's hands in turn. She had a very firm handshake indeed. It was as if she didn't want to let them go.

At last K J Sparkling stepped back and turned to Penny. "Now," she said. "This Award of yours – the *WOW!* Award for being Wonderful … Can we get on with it straightaway?"

"No problem," Penny smiled. "Everything's ready in our roof garden. Shall we all go up?"

"Not *all* of us, surely," said K J Sparkling.

"Sorry?"

K J Sparkling's voice had hardened for a moment, but when she spoke again it was as sweet as ever. "Not these lovely children here, Penny," she cooed. "Not if they want to be in my next book. That must be kept a secret. And people might guess if they see us together. Let me suggest another idea."

"Go on …?"

"Let *me* interview them for your magazine. We'll do it over lunch at my house here in the city. Just imagine! The kids who defeated Dr X in conversation with K J Sparkling. What do you think?"

What did they think?

"*WOW!*" said the children.

Maybe they *were* heroes, after all. Why else would the great K J Sparkling have been so nice to them?

Chapter 4 – Another arrival

K J Sparkling, Penny and Mum had all gone up to the roof garden for the award ceremony. Penny left the children with lots of old copies of *WOW!* to read, promising that they wouldn't be long.

Tiger sank on to the sofa and began to read. Cat also picked up a magazine. Max sat in Penny's swivel chair behind her desk and began to spin round.

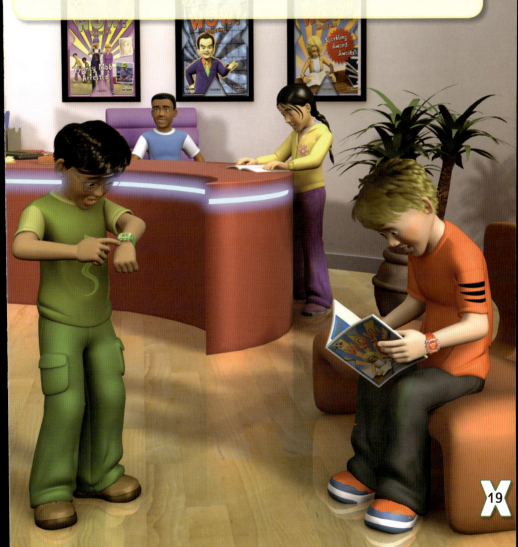

Ant was fiddling with his watch again. His fingers flicked over the buttons.

"What are you doing, Ant?" said Max, eventually.

"I was trying to tell you earlier, in the car …" he said, distracted.

"Tell us what?" said Cat, looking up from the magazine.

"My watch … I think I've discovered another function."

"What *function*?" scoffed Tiger.

"Time travel."

"TIME TRAVEL!" the others all laughed.

"Nice trick, Ant," said Tiger.

"Hey, what are you laughing at? It's not a trick. If I can just remember how to …"

BLIP!

Ant vanished.

BLIP!

Instantly, Ant was back. His eyes were wild with excitement. "You'll never guess what I've just seen ..."

"How did you –?" began Cat, but she was interrupted by the phone on Penny's desk which began to buzz.

"Answer it, Max," said Tiger.

"I'm not sure ..."

The phone buzzed again.

Finally, Max picked up Penny's phone.

"Hello?" said Max.

The others saw him blink in surprise as he listened.

"Err, you'd better send her up then. I'll tell Penny as soon as I get a chance ..." Slowly, he put down the handset. "It's K J Sparkling," he told them.

"K J Sparkling?" said Cat. "But she's upstairs."

"There's *another* K J Sparkling in the building. She says she's come to collect her award."

There was a soft knock at the door. Max got up from the chair and went to open it. In walked a lady with blonde hair that hid half her face. She looked round the room and smiled.

"Have I come to the right place?" she said.

"Are you K J Sparkling?" Cat asked.

"Yes, I am."

"And you're here for this year's *WOW!* Award?"

"That's right. I'm sorry to be so early but I couldn't wait any longer. I'm so excited about winning the vote in such a famous magazine. All sorts of wonderful things have happened to me since I started writing my books but this is the best of the lot. Are you Penny Piminy, the editor-in-chief?"

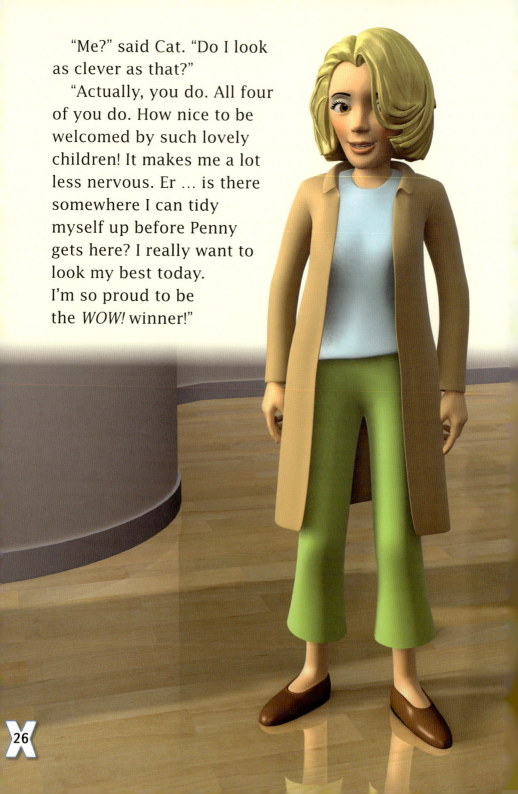

"Me?" said Cat. "Do I look as clever as that?"

"Actually, you do. All four of you do. How nice to be welcomed by such lovely children! It makes me a lot less nervous. Er … is there somewhere I can tidy myself up before Penny gets here? I really want to look my best today. I'm so proud to be the *WOW!* winner!"

"There's a cloakroom next door," said Max.

"That's just what I need. Will you excuse me for a moment? I'd love to hear all about you when I get back."

And before they knew it, she was gone.

The children stared at each other, open-mouthed. "Two K J Sparklings?" Cat exclaimed. "How can there be *two* K J Sparklings?"

"I'll tell you how," said Ant quietly. "That's if you're finally ready to listen to me!"

Chapter 6 – Time shift

Ant took a deep breath. "I tried to tell you before. I saw two K J Sparklings when I went back in time," he said. "One of them is an imposter!"

"An imposter? Why would anyone want to pretend to be K J Sparkling?" scoffed Tiger.

"Isn't it obvious?" said Ant. "Whoever the fake is, she's trying to take the *WOW!* Award for herself!"

"But ... but," stammered Cat. "They were both so *nice* and *wonderful*. Which is the real one?"

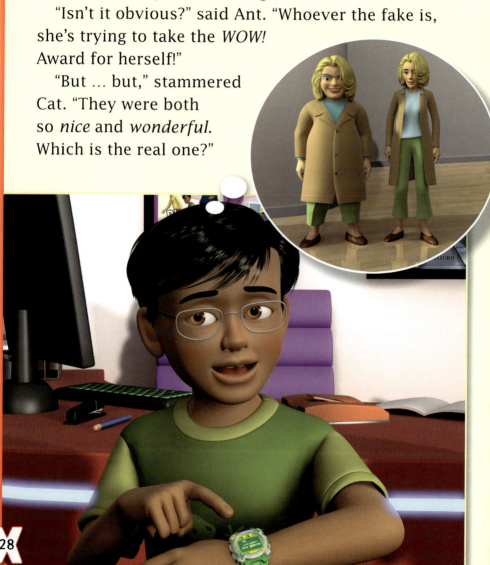

"I don't know," said Ant. "I couldn't tell."

Max looked thoughtful "So you're serious about this time travel thing, Ant?" he asked.

"Of course, I'm serious!" said Ant.

"Do you think we could all do it?"

"Well, I don't see why not. It's as simple as shrinking."

"Right," said Max. "Show us how, Ant. Then we can all slip back in time and take a look at each K J Sparkling as she arrives. Then we can find out who is the imposter and why she wants the award."

A few minutes later ...

"Everybody ready?" said Ant.

They turned the dials on their watches anticlockwise. The digital numbers began to flick backwards. They pushed another button and ...

BLIP! BLIP! BLIP! BLIP!

They were standing in the shadows outside of the WOW! building. In front of them, a bike pulled up next to the kerb. K J Sparkling got off of it. As she was locking her bike, a child ran up to her holding out a notepad and pen. K J smiled and signed an autograph.

… BLIP! BLIP! BLIP! BLIP!

Now the children were in the same place but twenty minutes earlier. A big purple car had just arrived. Two men got out of the front. They were wearing purple suits that were a perfect match with the car itself. The children recognized them instantly.

"It's Plug and Socket!" Cat hissed.

"So who's that sitting in the back?" asked Tiger.

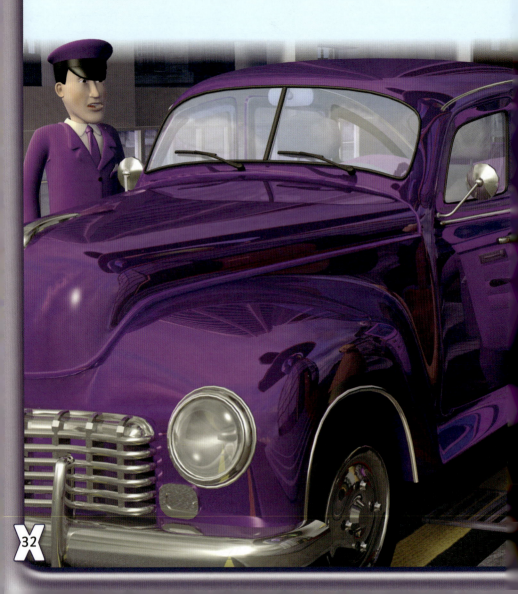

Plug held the door open and the other K J Sparkling got out. She was shorter than the one they'd just seen, and rounder. As she stepped out of the car and on to the pavement, her hair slipped to one side.

"A wig!" said Max.

The fake K J Sparkling straightened her hair, twisted her face into a smile and swept up the steps to the main entrance.

... BLIP! BLIP! BLIP! BLIP!

Back in the present, in Penny's office, there was a long moment before any of the children spoke.

"So much for wanting to interview us," said Cat eventually.

"So much for us being in the next best-seller!" huffed Tiger.

"But we still don't know who she is," said Ant.

"Don't we?" said Max

"What do you mean?" asked Cat.

"Do you remember the story Miss Jones told us about Beowulf and the monster Grendel? After Grendel finally lost the fight, who was it who came out of the swamp to sort Beowulf out?"

"His mum?"

"Exactly," said Max, grimly.

"You think Dr X's mum is behind this?" asked Cat.

"You can usually rely on your mum to help you out in an emergency. In this case, Dr X's mum must be standing in for him while he's in prison. She hasn't come out of a swamp, though. I bet that purple limo brought her straight from NASTI."

"Maybe she wants the *WOW!* Award to give to Dr X?" suggested Ant.

"Or maybe she's come for the watches," said Tiger. "That's why she wanted to interview us afterwards!"

Chapter 7 – The *WOW!* Award for being Wonderful

Max took charge of the situation. His orders were crisp and clear. "Cat, phone the police. Ask for Inspector Textor," he said. "When he arrives, bring them up to the roof garden."

"What are you going to do?" asked Cat.

"We'll do our best to hold up the award ceremony."

The lift had an OUT OF ORDER sign on the door. So Max, Ant and Tiger took the stairs, bounding up them two-at-a-time.

When they burst through the doors of the roof garden, the presentation was almost over. Mrs X was making a speech, talking into a crackly microphone.

"Thank you so much, *WOW!*" said Mrs X. "The *WOW!* Award for being Wonderful is definitely going to the right person. I'll keep it safe till my son … err … till some*one* gives me something better. Now, if you'll hand it over – "

"No!" Tiger howled.

"Keep hold of it, Penny!" yelled Ant.

Mrs X spun round. She snatched the *WOW!* Award from the flabbergasted Penny. Then, before anyone could stop her, she clambered on to the low wall that surrounded the roof garden.

"Stop," Max yelled. "Don't jump!"

"Jump?" she snarled. "Do you think I'm mad?"

There was nothing shy and gentle about her now. She tore off her wig and flung it away. Then she turned one of the buttons on the front of her coat. From out the back of it, helicopter blades appeared. She tugged a cord and the blades began to rotate.

"See?" she screeched. "Only an idiot forgets to plan for a fast getaway. I'll sort you brats out another time."

Her feet were hovering just above the parapet.

Just then, a figure on the edge of the crowd sprung forwards. Max gawped. He had never seen his mum move so fast. With a giant leap, she caught Mrs X by the ankle. Mrs X let out a scream of fury. Max's mum simply gritted her teeth and held on.

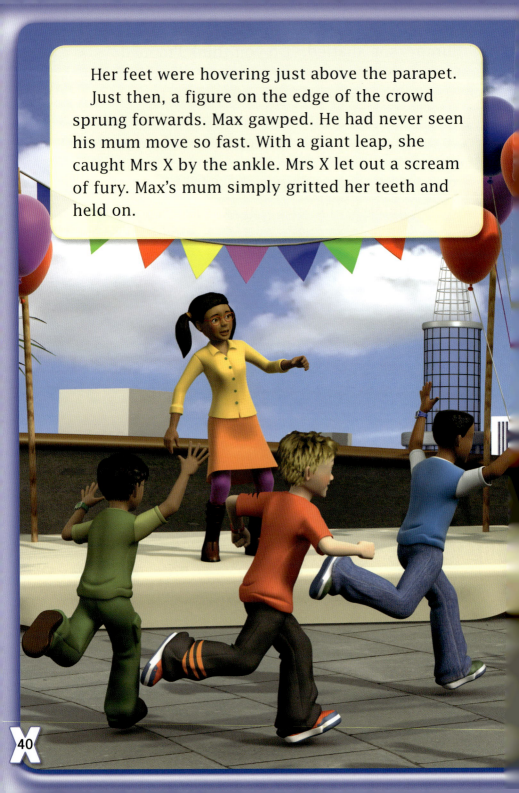

Mrs X hovered in mid-air, close to the edge of the building, with Max's mum hanging beneath.

"MUM!" yelled Max, as he grabbed her.

Other people were joining in now helping to pull his mum and Mrs X back from the brink.

Mum and Mrs X landed just as Inspector Textor and his police squad burst on to the roof. Cat followed closely behind.

Mrs X was put in handcuffs while Inspector Textor politely lifted Max's mum to her feet. "Are you all right, Ma'am?" he asked.

"I'm fine, Officer," she said. "I was just doing what mums do ... helping out in an emergency!"

"Oh, dear! Am I too late?" said K J Sparkling, blushing, as she appeared at the top of the steps. "I'm so sorry, but I got locked in the bathroom. Then I got lost coming up here …"

"It's OK," said Penny, rushing forwards to meet her. "We're running a bit late anyway." Penny quickly explained what had happened.

"Oh, my!" exclaimed K J Sparkling. "What a great story! You children are so brave." She was thoughtful for a moment. "Do you know," she said. "I might just put you in my next book!"

Max's mum didn't miss out either. K J Sparkling was so impressed that she asked Penny if Max's mum could keep the *WOW!* Award for being Wonderful instead of her. Penny happily agreed.

Chapter 8 – The best *WOW!* ever

It was a special edition all right. In fact, everyone agreed it was the best edition of *WOW!* ever. It was packed with exciting stories about the children, about Dr X and K J Sparkling.

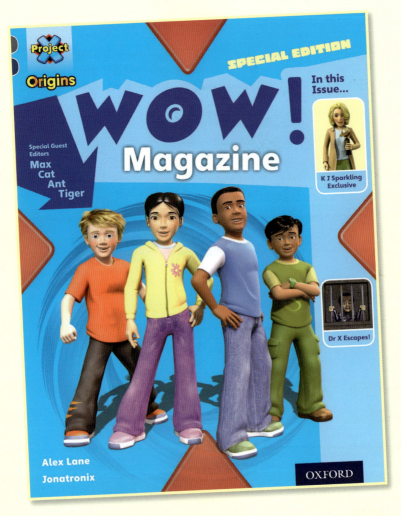

Of course, the micro-friends kept the bit about their watches safe and secret! *Blip!*

Later that day ...

In Greenville City Jail, Dr X and his mum were catching up.

GREENVILLE NEWS

X Escapes!

The famous criminal Dr X has escaped! "He was there when I locked up last night," said his guard, Joe Malone. "But when I checked this morning, he had gone! I don't know how he got out."

The mystery deepens because Dr X's mum, Mrs X, who was recently arrested for trying to steal the *WOW!* Award for being Wonderful, was still in the cell. She is refusing to talk about what happened. Inspector Textor has asked the people of Greenville to be on their guard. Who knows what he might do next?